# Mel Bay Prese

# Mandolin
# Classics in
# Tablature

## By Robert Bancalari

# CONTENTS

# SONATA NO. 7
## Op. 5

**Preludio**

I

Arcangelo Corelli
(1653–1713)

4

## II

**Corrente**

**Allegro**

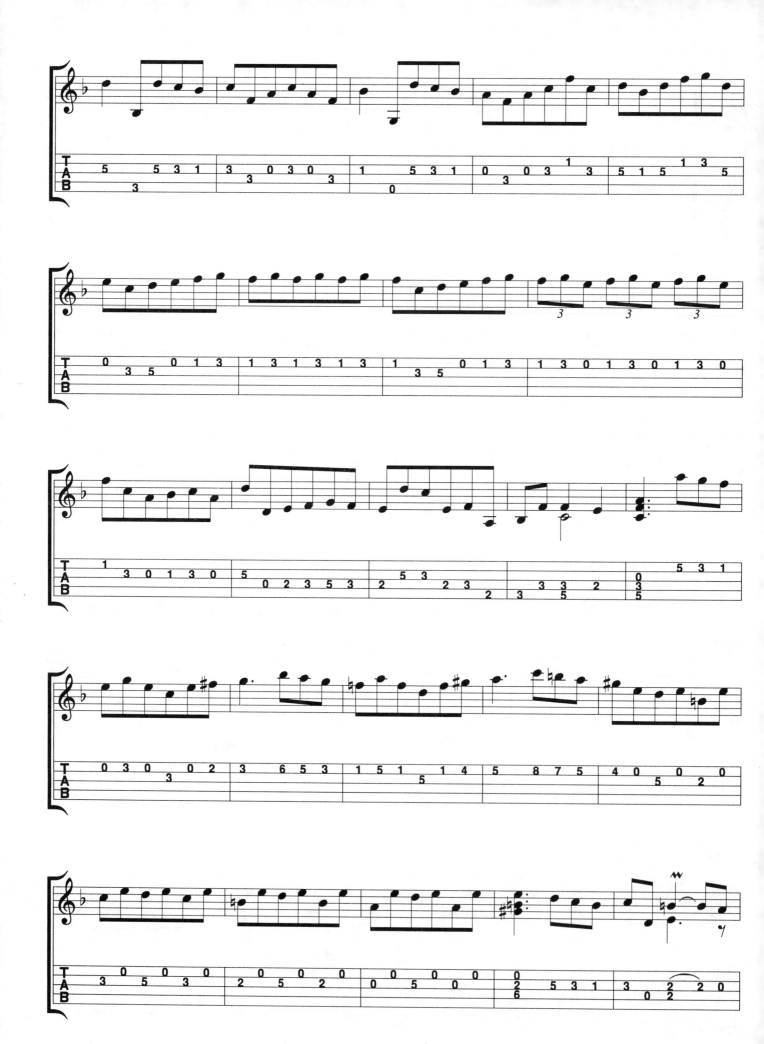

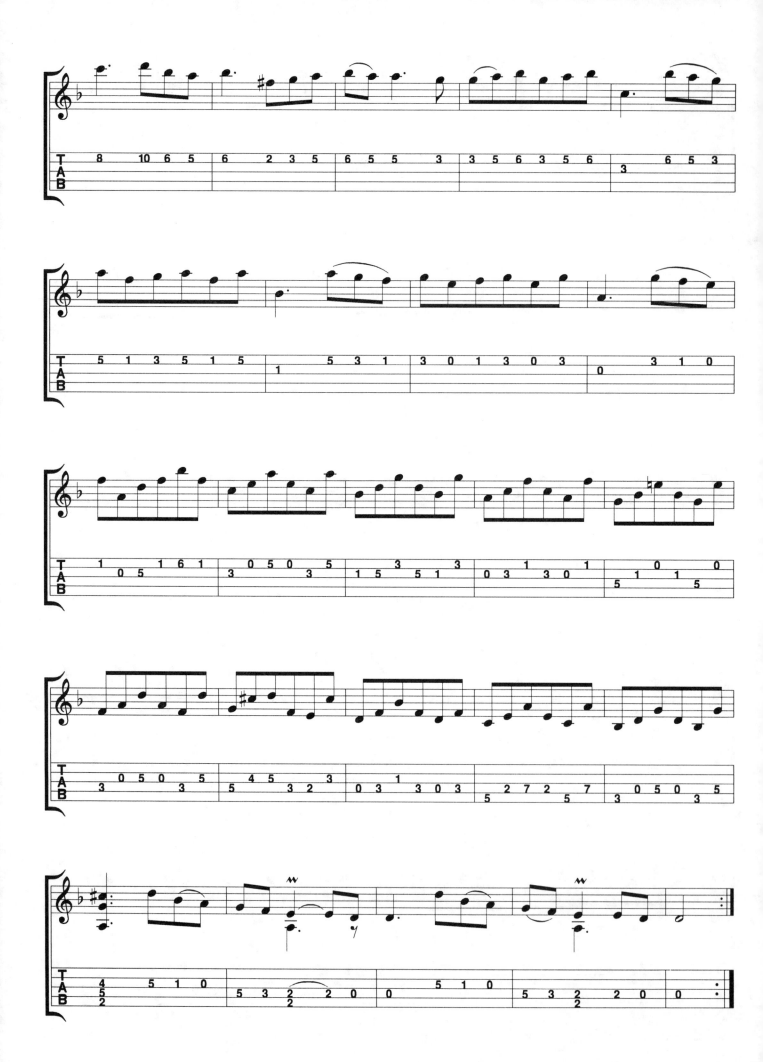

# III

Sarabanda

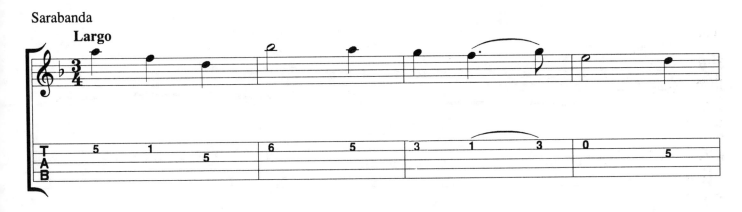

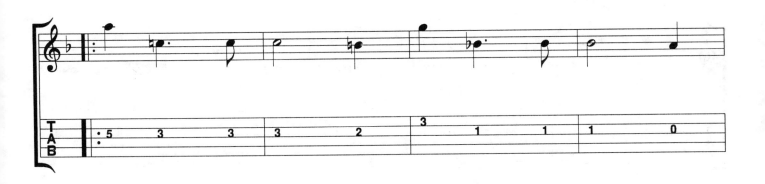

# IV

Giga

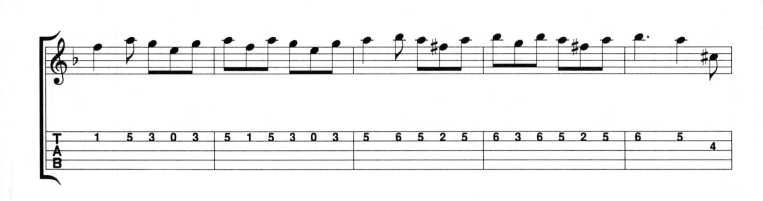

# SONATA NO. 14

## Op. 1

### I

G. F. Handel
(1685–1759)

II

# IV

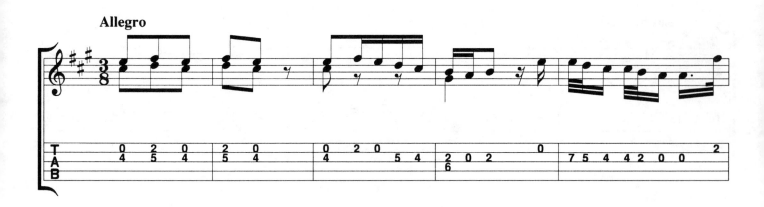

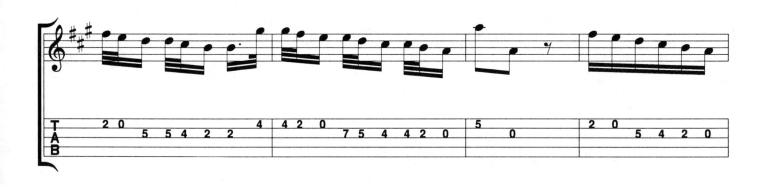

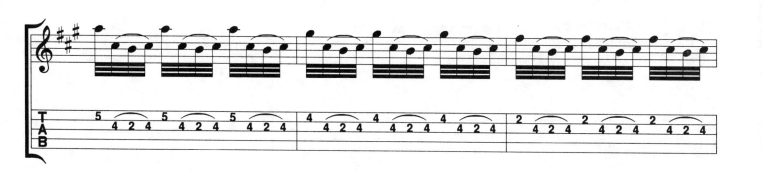

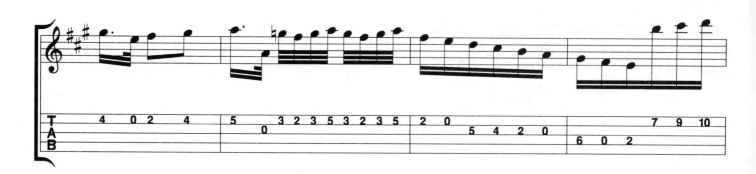

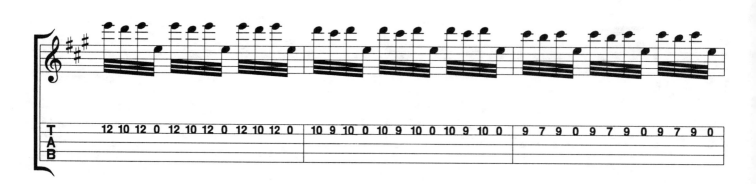

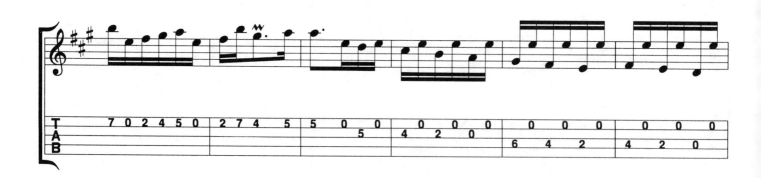

# FANTASIE

## I

G. P. Telemann
(1681–1767)

23

II

Grave

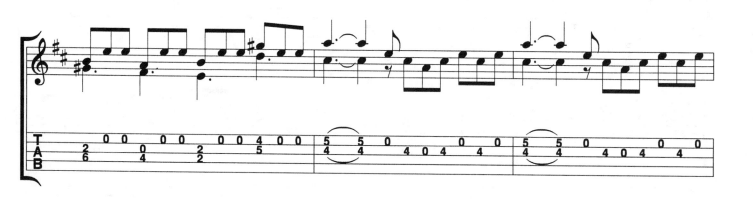

26

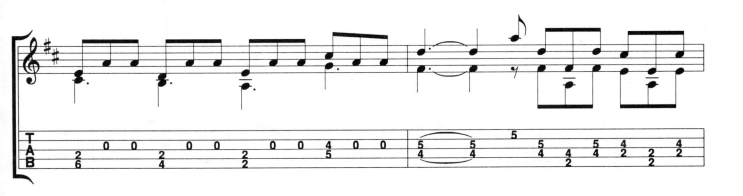

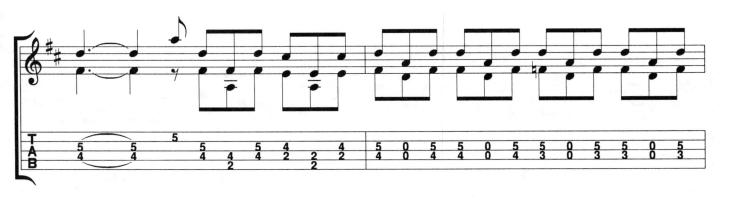

# ANGLAISE
## (From French Suite #3)

J. S. Bach
(1685–1750)

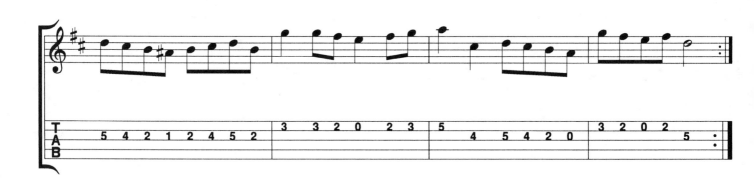

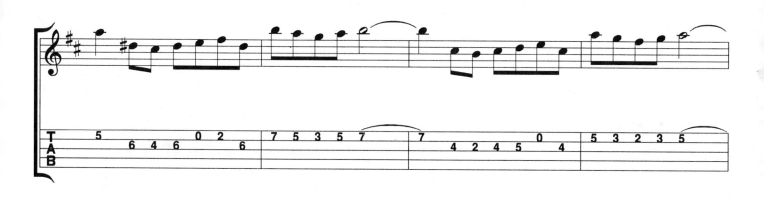

# ALLEMANDE

Thomas Baltzer
(ca. 1630–1663)

# SONATA DA CHIESA
## (Op. 5 #3)
### I & II Movements

### I

Arcangelo Corelli
(1653–1713)

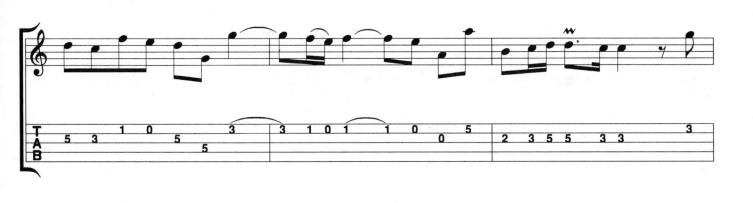

## II

36

# HORN PIPE

Henry Purcell
(1659–1695)

# LES PAPILLONS

François Couperin
(1668–1733)

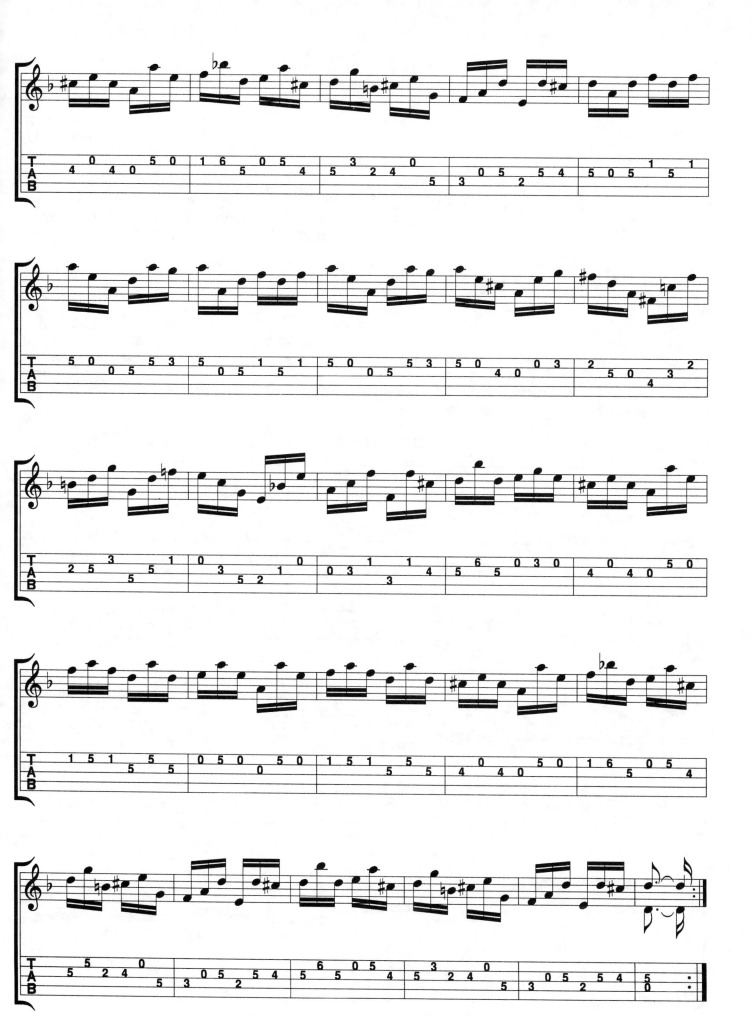

# PRELUDE

J. S. BACH
(1685–1750)

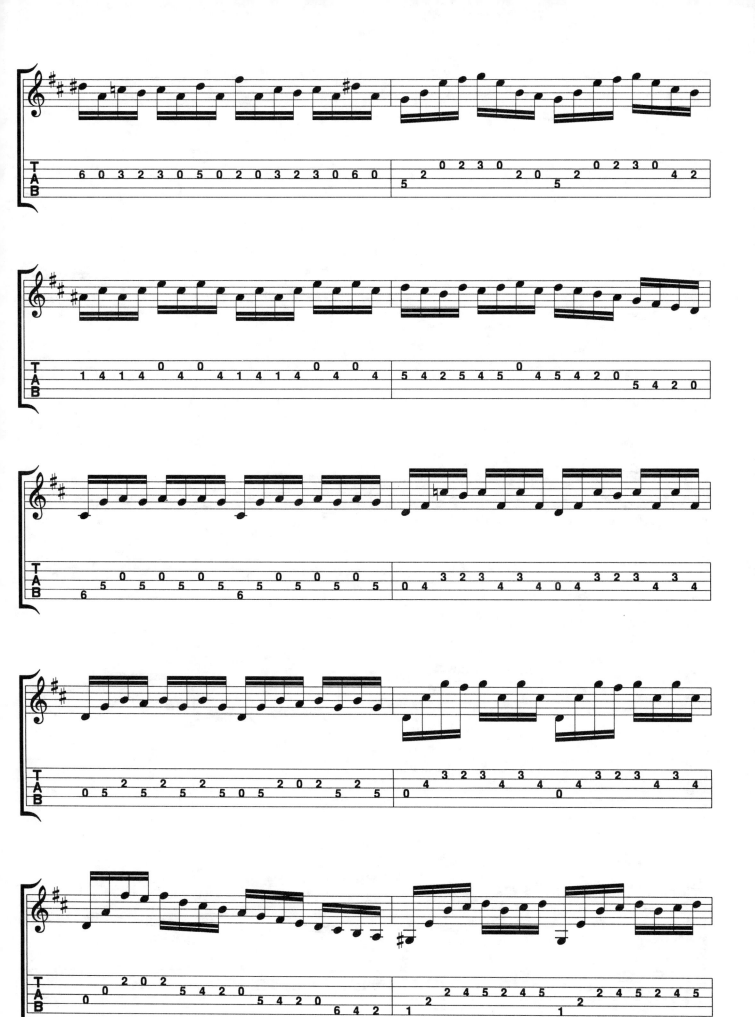

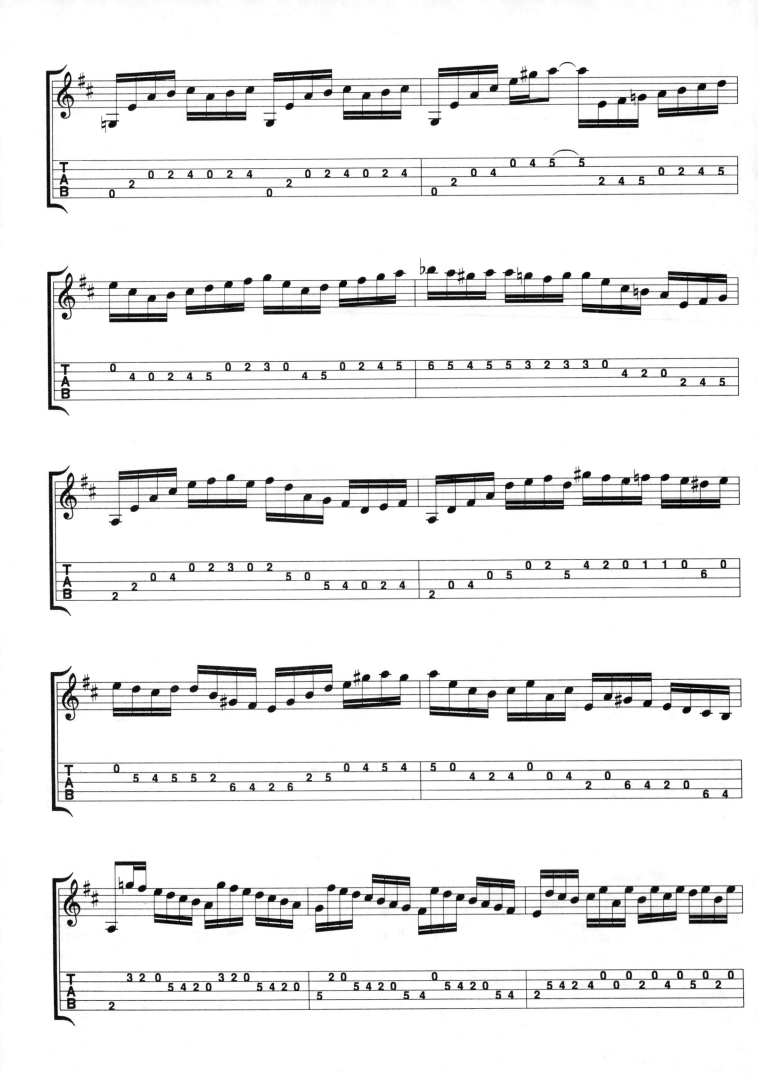

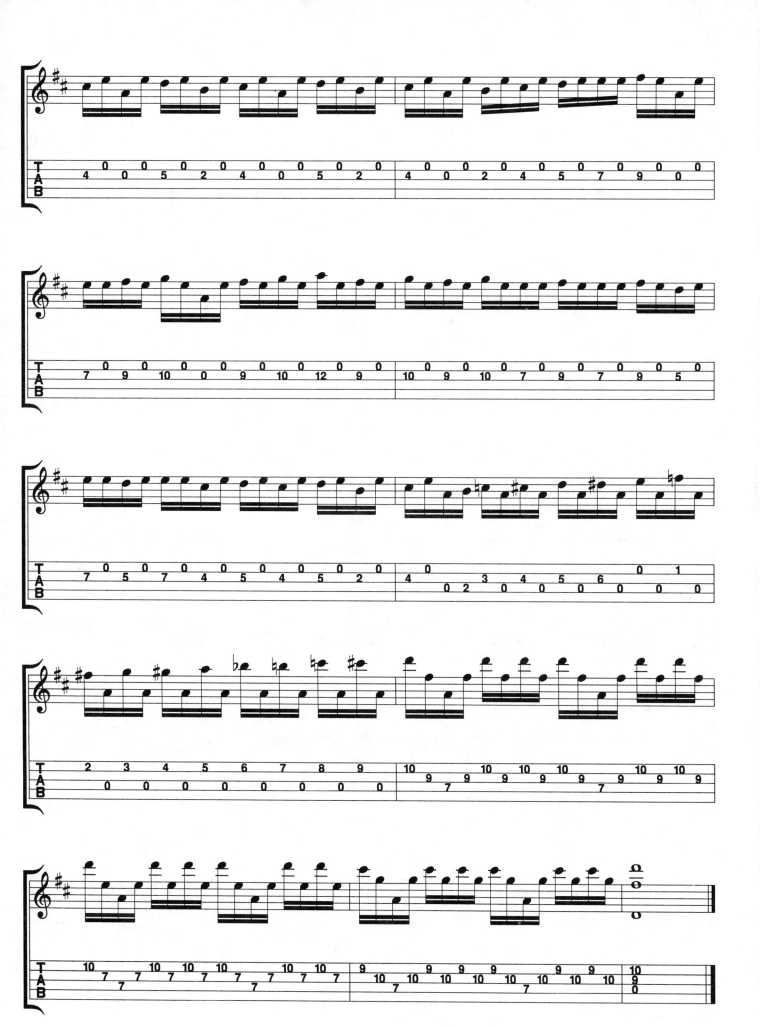

# GIGA

J. S. Bach
(1685-1750)

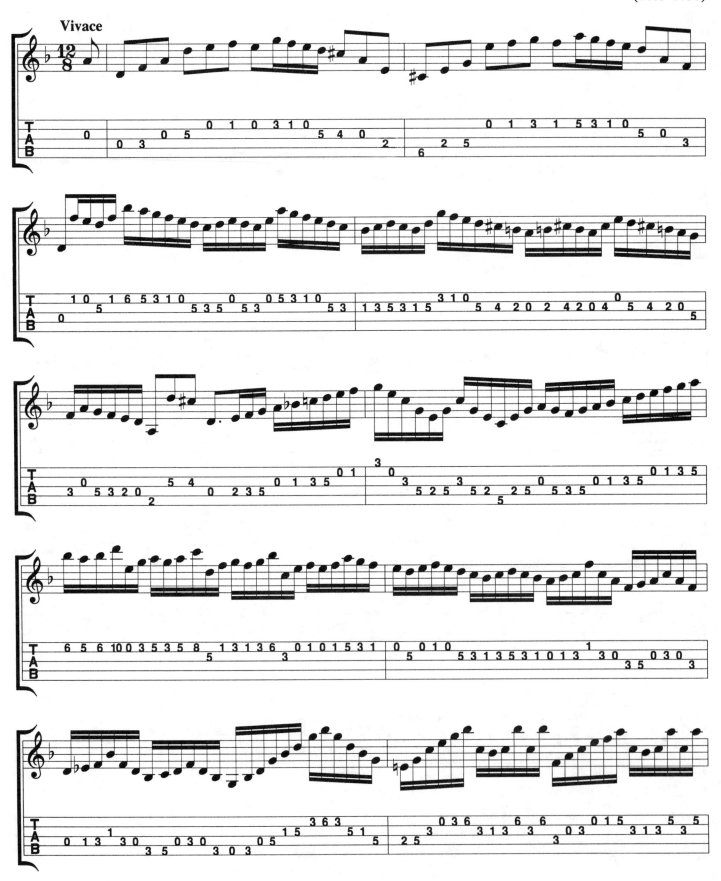

44

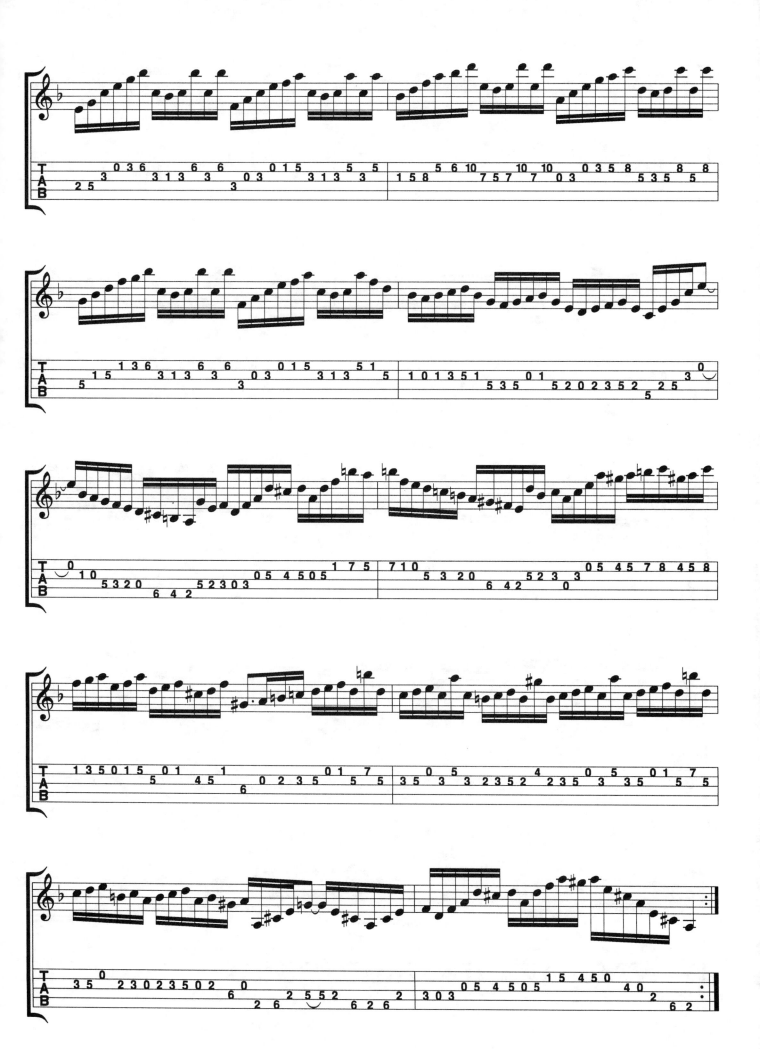

45

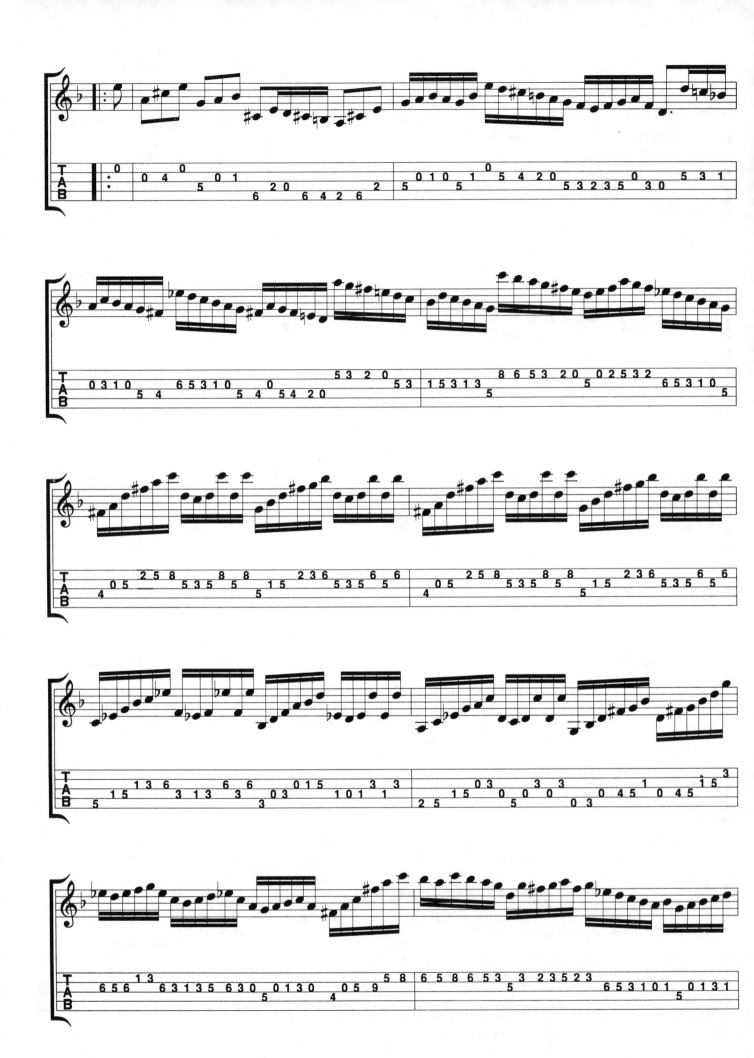

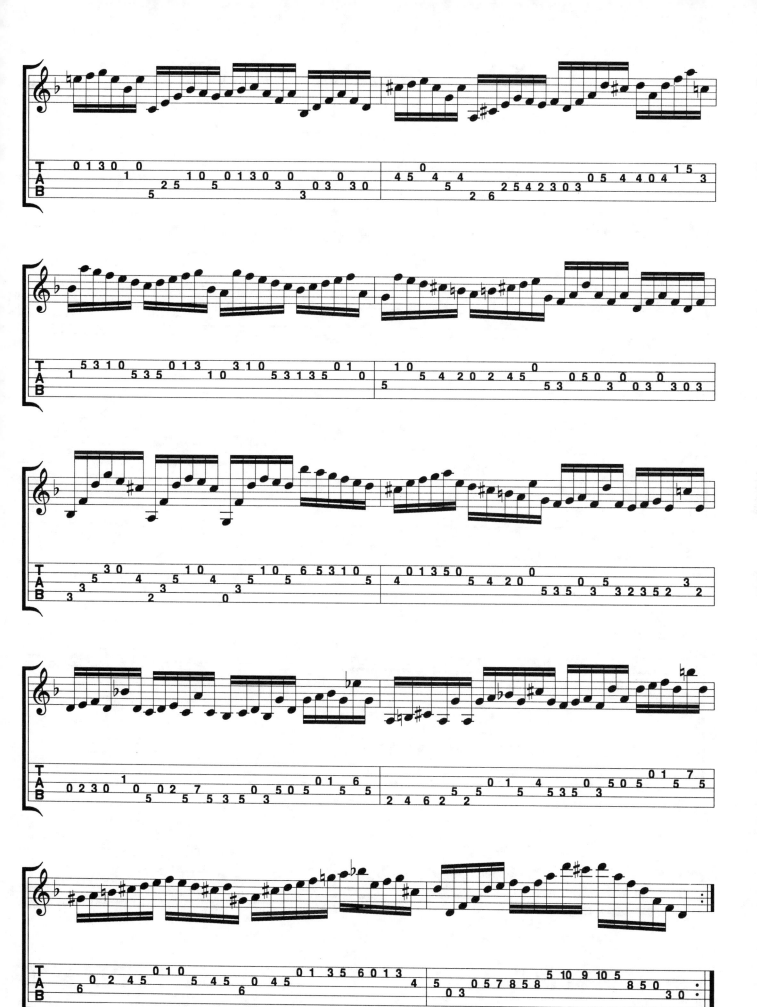

47

# CONCERTO IN A MINOR

## Op. 3 No. 6

### (III Movement)

Antonio Vivaldi
(CA. 1675–1741)

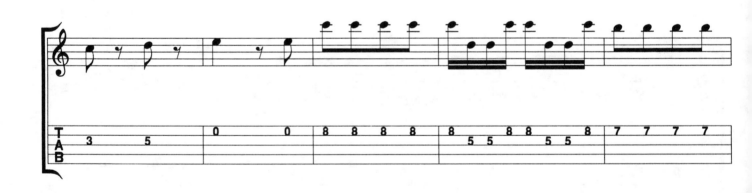

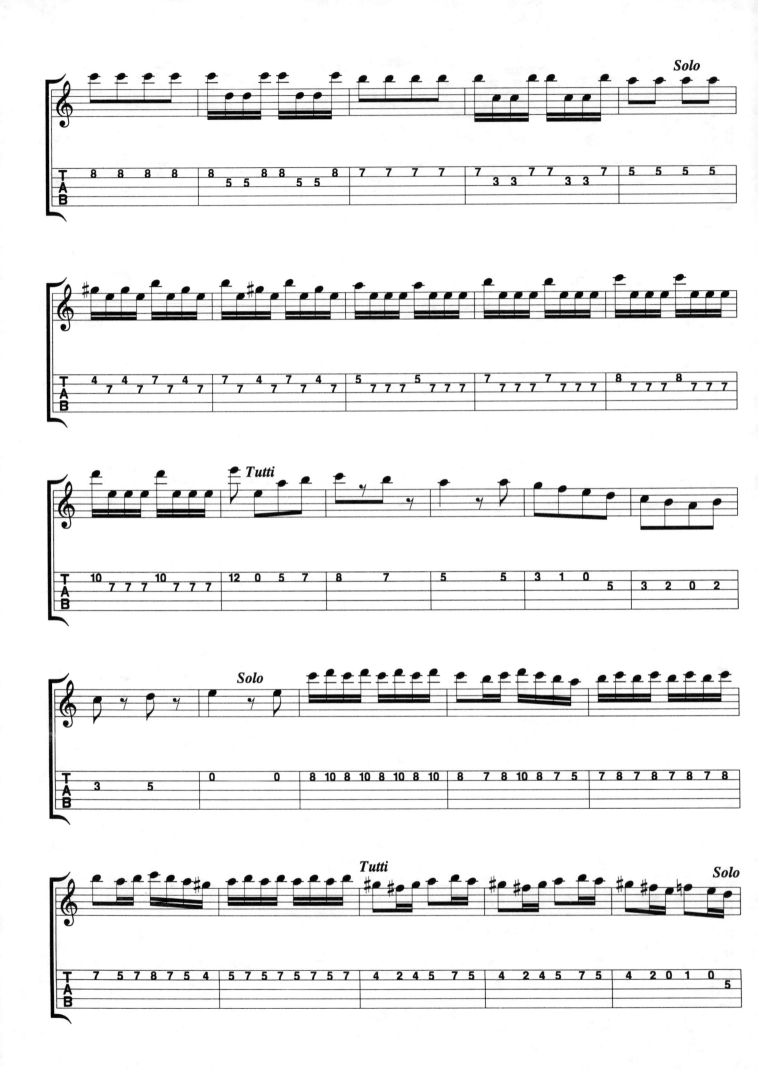

*Great Music at Your Fingertips*